Ulrich Frey

A brief outline of The Philosophy of Freedom by Rudolf Steiner

Translated from the original German
by Norman Skillen

Herstellung und Verlag:
BoD – Books on Demand, Norderstedt
ISBN: 978-3-7504-8234-0

Preface

This piece of writing is a study guide for readers of Rudolf Steiner's *Philosophy of Freedom*. It was originally intended for my own personal use, but, encouraged by positive reactions to it, I decided to publish it in 2007. Sustained demand and my own changing needs then motivated me to revise and hopefully improve the text as an outline of the original and an aid to understanding it.

The philosophical issues of the day have not featured in the text in any particular way. At the end, as an aid to reflection, the main ideas of each chapter have been individually formulated.

Since this resumée is really only a sketch, it is not a suitable basis upon which to form a judgement of the original. Those for whom doing this is too much trouble can at least get a broad outline here. I would hope, however, that they would still, at some time, give this sublime and beautiful work of Rudolf Steiner's the attention it deserves.

U. Frey

I Conscious human action

Can human beings do, or not do, whatever they want? In other words, are they completely self-determined in their actions, or externally determined perhaps without noticing. In 1674 the philosopher Spinoza gave this example to illustrate this question: if a stone receives an impact such that it moves forwards, it could mistakenly think that it is moving under its own impetus. Exactly the same is true of a child craving milk, or a boy swearing revenge. Both assume they are self-motivated, but fail to notice that they are being led by other causes, namely hunger or anger. The objection may be raised here that action based upon consciously recognised motives cannot be regarded as equivalent to that of a hungry or an angry child.

According to Eduard von Hartmann human action is determined by a person's character. It is only through character that an idea becomes an impulse to action. Certain ideas compel a person to act, because they fit with his character. Here also the fact that the impulse to action can be permeated with consciousness is not taken into account. If there is a difference between a consciously recognised motive for my action and an unconscious impulse, such as hunger, anger etc., then in each case the resultant action should be evaluated differently. Thus action motivated by knowledge should be granted the special significance it deserves. For if reason, or a decision based on insight, exert the same compulsion upon us as do animal drives like hunger and anger, then we cannot speak of freedom. If some motivational impulse arising from my character is urging me to do something, even though I can see that it is irrational, then I should be glad that I can refrain from putting this willed, if undesired, impulse into practice. The point is not whether we can carry out a decision we have made, but how the decision takes shape in us. If we do not know why we are doing something, then this action cannot be regarded as free.

II   The fundamental desire to know

The human being is never content with what he finds before him, but always strives for something beyond it. This goes for the act of knowing as well. It is not enough for us to simply perceive with the senses, we also want to be able to explain the phenomena we have experienced. Our experience is dual – of things, on the one hand, and of ourselves on the other. In this way we distinguish ourselves as independent beings from the world of things, thus creating the antithesis of Self and world. We nonetheless feel connected to the world, that we are beings in the world. Our intellectual and spiritual aspirations arise through our wishing to overcome these opposite feelings of simultaneous separation from and connection to the world. This can be accomplished in various ways. The religious person seeks unity by means of divine revelation, the artist through creative action, by which she imbues matter with her ideas thus reconciling her inner life with the outer world. The philosopher too does not stop at the phenomenon, but tries to penetrate what has been observed with thinking.

To restore the connection to the world from which our awareness of our separate identity has detached us, the content of the world has to become the content of thought.

Two worldviews have tried to bridge this gulf in different ways: dualism, as a two-world theory, has not been able to find the bridge between mind and matter; monism, as a unitary view of the world, refuses to recognise the contraries involved – either, as materialism, it denies mind, or as idealism / spiritualism, matter.

We may have torn ourselves away from nature, but in doing so we have taken something of her with us. It is this aspect belonging to her that connects us and makes us feel we belong to her. The first thing to be done, then, is to find this aspect of nature within us, for only by gaining knowledge of nature as she lives in us can we discover her outside ourselves.

III   Thinking in the service of our conception of the world

If I observe a process in the external world, it proceeds independently of me. As soon as I begin applying conceptual understanding to the process, I become active and notice things going on that I previously did not know. In contrast to the process itself, its conceptualising is an activity dependent upon me. Whether I do this or not is entirely up to me. Either way, it has no effect upon the course of the process.

However, if I saturate my observations with thought, the course of such independent processes becomes predictable for me.

Observation is the fundamental prerequisite of all experience, because only by observing something can I become aware of it. But observation alone creates no concepts, no explanations of experience. It is only by combining the observed with thinking that I arrive at knowledge of what particular observations might mean. Thus, observation and thinking are the starting points of all intellectual and spiritual striving.

As a rule thinking is directed towards an object of observation. This is what renders it imperceptible, because while thinking is proceeding attention is upon the object of thought and not upon thinking itself. It can, however, be directed towards itself. Thinking itself can, as it were, become the object of thought-filled observation. This mode of observation, however, is the exception, since objects and processes are normally what are observed, and not the actual thinking that explains them.

Nor is it possible for me to observe my thinking as it is happening. I am only capable of making the experience resulting from my thinking an object of observation after the fact. To catch thinking in the act would mean observing the activity used to observe it. If we add thinking to the list of observables, we have increased the number of observable objects, but not the number of observation methods. Since everything, apart from thinking, exists without any action on our part, we experience everything, except thinking, as enigmatic. For in thinking about thinking activity and object are one and the same. Thinking is independent of everything else, it exists through itself. In world development thinking appeared last, which is why in seeking to explain the former we must begin with the latter. Only with thinking do we know how it is done. Therefore thinking itself must first be understood, for it is the tool of knowledge.

IV The world as percept

To sense impressions thinking adds an ideationall counterpart. If the object disappears form the perceptual field, its ideationall counterpart still exists in my memory. That which remains in my memory is the concept of the object.

A concept does not exist by and for itself, it links up with other concepts to form a coherent whole. Thus, for instance, the concept "organism" is related to the concepts of "growth" and "reproduction". These connections create a conceptual system, which, according to my level of experience, will be more or less complete, and will be extended as my experience grows. An idea is more substantial, more comprehensive than a concept, usually encompassing many concepts and their relationships and mutual dependencies. Ideas and concepts are acquired by thinking, not by observing. Observation and concept meet in the human mind and are there joined together. Human consciousness is the mediator between thinking and observation. If my thinking is directed towards an object, then I am conscious of this object. If my thinking is directed towards myself, then I am conscious of myself. Thus thinking is bound neither to the object nor the subject; it forms both these concepts as it does all others, and is therefore not purely subjective. Thinking leads me beyond my Self and brings me into contact with objects. On the other hand it places me opposite these objects as subject. In this consists the dual nature of the human being.

Let us consider the world of pure sensation, which presents itself to us in the absence of any effects of thought. As external world we perceive a host of colours and forms, sounds, smells etc., which make up a diffuse aggregate of sensed objects on the level of pure sensation. We are aware of feelings, likewise devoid of any order. This is the world of experience minus concepts, in which one sense impression merges into another in space and time, one feeling replaces another, without our having the slightest inkling why or wherefore.

Perception is a different matter when thinking is calling the shots, linking concepts one to another and bringing them into relationship with each other. Then we know why the one thing follows the other, what functions particular things have, and how they mutually influence and condition each other.

These connections between things which thinking brings to light are not just subjectively valid, but also generally.

What I perceive is initially dependent on me. On the one hand, it is a question of where I am, but on the other also of my bodily and mental organisation. Thus for a blind person, for instance, visual perception is missing from the world of his experience.

What then is the function of our perceptual activity in the taking shape of a percept. Of that which has been perceived what was already there before we perceived it, and what is an object of perception in and of itself?

The perceptions of external things come and go. By contrast, the perception of myself as subject remains. In myself as subject the perceptions of things remain as mental images or representations. I perceive mental images in my mind, like colours or sounds in connection with the objects of the external world.

Now, is the object really as I see it in my mind, or is it altered by my process of perception? Perhaps the representation I have of something does not tally with the *thing in itself.*

Let us, therefore, follow the path of a sensory stimulus from the outer world via a sense organ into the brain, where it is said to become conscious to us as a sensation. We look at a table. In being perceived this table evokes various electrical and chemical reactions on our retina. These reactions are transmitted through the optic nerve to a specific region of the posterior cortex. This is the last instance where we can detect bodily reactions to the external sensory stimulus, in this case, the table. We do not, however, perceive the table as such in the said region of the brain, rather in our consciousness the various sensory impressions are united as representation to the external object. This representation, however, is thought to have nothing in common with the object itself, since it has been entirely changed by the process of perception on its journey though the body, in this case from eye to brain. Then it must also be taken into account that we can only track the sense impression of the table as far as the cortex, and that the transitional pathway from the last brain process to the outwardly perceived table is interrupted. If, therefore, the table only exists for me as a representation, which is assumed to have nothing to do with the *table in itself*, because it was altered on its way into the brain, what right do I have to assert that the eye, optic nerve and brain are real and not exactly like my mental images of them, which have nothing to do with the *eye, optic nerve and brain in themselves.*

In this manner so-called critical idealism seeks to show that it is impossible to determine what happens to a sense impression during the process of perception, because it regards the things of the external world as subjective representations, and the body, by contrast, as objective fact.

V Knowledge of the world

Critical idealism, as just shown, has no force in argument, because it refutes its own premises. If all perceived objects are supposed to be mere representations, then the sense organs cannot be regarded as real, but only as representations. Why should they be treated differently to all other things? If it is true that we cannot perceive things as they really are, that they are not directly accessible to our observation, then for us to have any knowledge of things at all would mean our having recourse to our mental images of them.

This is the path followed by modern science. It uses sense perception as the last resort in the effort to acquire knowledge of the processes going on in the *things in themselves* behind what the senses perceive. For science the truth is to be found in these processes that are not accessible to the senses.

The critical idealist attempts to use the representation in his philosophical quest for knowledge of the nature of being. But the notion of the *thing in itself* must also be designated as a representation. From this perspective even one's own personal identity can only be a product of representation. Thus, according to this absolute illusionism, personal identity also becomes merely a dream image.

Transcendental realism, as propounded by Eduard von Hartmann, purports to be able to draw conclusions about the true nature of things from their representations.

Someone waking from a dream does not think about it according to the laws of the dream-world, but those of the real world. Even the interpreter of dreams makes use of the knowledge he has from waking consciousness. As dream is to waking, so is mere sensation to thinking. Only with the help of thinking can anything be predicated of perception. Thinking insinuates itself between the percepts. The object, as a percept, is not a totality, to which thinking is subsequently added. It is only though the elements of thinking and perception that the object as a whole, including its concept, becomes available to our mental organisation.

A human subject can only perceive a very limited extract of the totality of all things. Out of the universal system of inter-related concepts reason only has particular concepts at its disposal.

My self-awareness places me within certain limits. My thinking, however, has nothing to do with these limits. It regulates my limited existence, as it does all other existence, from a higher sphere. In contrast to my individual feeling, my thinking is universal.

Thus there is only one concept of a triangle, although it will be construed differently by the mind of each individual. Mind itself is one. In thinking we unite our individuality with the cosmos to form a single whole. In feeling we experience a part of the cosmos in ourselves in an individual way.

Mind is an all-pervasive power. We first encounter it, not as something flowing out from the centre of the cosmos, but at a point on the periphery, namely in our own individual consciousness – otherwise we would know all the riddles of the world in the moment of becoming conscious. Thinking reaches out beyond our limited existence to the universal being of the cosmos. The possibility of overcoming the limits of our existence is what gives us our desire for knowledge, a desire which only thinking beings have. The concept ignites where mind makes contact with the external object. Knowledge establishes balance between inner and outer, that is, between the concept and the object. What is common to all individual beings in this world is not a personal God, as proclaimed by various religious denominations, not force or matter as science teaches, nor the indeterminate will as described by Schopenhauer, but the Ideal.

Thinking is not abstract. Without thinking the world of sense perception would be an aggregate of unconnected objects, mere juxtaposition in space and a linear succession of separate moments in time. Thinking is what connects the threads from one being to another, evaluating individual percepts in the process, and revealing their interrelationships. This is a meaningful activity. The content of perception is given to us from without, thought content appears within. In the form it takes on its first appearance within us, this thought content may be called intuition. This thought content is to thinking what observation is to perception. In combination these two form the source of knowledge.

Intuition gives us access to the whole of reality. Through it the object, previously separated out by our mental organisation, is re-integrated into the universal whole.

Any subject-object relationship that goes beyond the perceptible can only be ideal. Connections between percepts can only be brought to light by thought. Only thinking forges the bond between the subjective and the objective. The perceived object changes my subjective state. The possibility remains of recalling the object, say, a table, to memory. This recollection, then, is the representation of the table, in other words, the subjective percept. The actual table, on the other hand, is perceived objectively. Now we know where in the perceptual field the representation is to be found, but its exact concept still escapes us. The latter, then, can reveal to us the relationship between representation and object.

VI   Human individuality

I, myself, with everything that makes up my character, am just as much a part of the generality of world events as any other object. The forces acting in my body are the same as those at work in the external world. In this respect, I am just like all other things. For perception, both my body and things in general belong to the same world totality. If an extract of this world impinges on me, if, in other words, I have a particular perception, thinking is simultaneously activated by me and an element in my cognitive system, a particular intuition, a concept unites with the percept. When the percept itself has disappeared, this union remains as a representation. This representation is the intuition cognate with this percept, it is an individualised concept, through which the reality of things is represented for us. The representation stands between percept and concept and, as such, is the concept pointing towards the corresponding percept. The sum of everything of which I can form representations constitutes my experience. If I were only concerned with knowledge, then the objective would extend no further than percept, concept and representation. What I perceive, however, is not only referred by thinking to the concept, but also to my own particular brand of subjectivity, my individual Self. This referencing of Self is expressed as a feeling – of pleasure or displeasure.

In thinking we participate in the general activities of the world, in feeling we withdraw back into ourselves. In approaching the Self purely in the mode of knowledge we would be completely indifferent to ourselves. It is only when this is complemented by feeling, by the experience of pleasure or pain, that we reach beyond the mere concept of ourselves to become individuals imbued with feeling. For the individual the life of feeling may even have more real meaning, but in feeling devoid of thought the world would lose its meaning altogether. Parallel to that of knowledge, the life of feeling also requires schooling and development.

VII   Are there limits to knowledge?

The act of knowing overcomes the duality with which an object initially presents itself to me. It fuses perception and its thought-engendered concept together into the object as a whole. For the subject the world is initially given as a duality (dualistic), and through the process of knowing is converted into a unity (monistic). The so-called *thing in itself* (*"Ding an sich"*), in other words an assumed something lying behind our perception, is an unjustified hypothesis, since the assumption is imposed upon the realm of percept and concept from outside it. Everything needed to explain a phenomenon in the world lies in the world itself. Acquisition of knowledge is only hindered by individual deficiencies. There are no universal limits to knowledge, only individual ones. Not until the thinking Self has bridged the separation between percept and concept it originally created have the demands of knowledge been satisfied. Hindrances to knowledge are transitory, they can be overcome through progress in perception and thinking. For us the concept is the only form the relationships between individual percepts mediated by thinking can take.

Perception, however, is not confined to the senses. Within the context of the mind and our inner life we may also speak of percepts. It goes for these too that their concept first has to be arrived at by thinking, if we are ever to know their reality.

VIII   The factors of life

We have already seen that the world presents itself initially as a multiplicity, a sum of individual things, and that the human being herself is one of these. We encounter everything, including ourselves, as mere percept, and also perceive ourselves as one percept among others. Nevertheless, in the middle of this perception of ourselves something appears which connects us to the other percepts. This something is not a mere percept. Nor is it something we simply encounter, but is produced by action on our part. It leads us beyond ourselves, and to each individual percept it adds ideal, inter-related modifications. The Self likewise undergoes ideal modification becoming a distinct subject or "I" standing in contrast to objects. This something is thinking, and the ideal modifications are concepts and ideas. However, the establishing of purely ideational relationships between percepts and between ourselves and the percepts by no means exhausts our capabilities. We are beings, not merely capable of knowing, but also of feeling and willing.

The ideal is operative not only in our relating percepts to ourselves in thinking, but also in feeling. With the former the ideal modification is objective in nature, whereas feeling remains a purely individual act. In feeling we have individual experience of the relation of external objects to ourselves as subject, whereas in willing we are aware of the individual relation of the Self to the objective world.

Therefore neither feeling nor will can be considered universal principles. They are actually only percepts, just like everything else. If feeling is declared a principle of knowledge as with the mystic, or will a universal principle as with the philosopher of will, then it is simply being asserted that a part of the immediately perceptible world is the whole of reality. This is just as insufficient as naïve realism's assumption that immediate sense perception gives us the full reality.

The desire to arrive at the essence of reality through something other than thinking arises because the concreteness of thinking easily slips from our attention. And all the while this concrete, living thinking also possesses intense elements of feeling and will; and it is precisely because it is so incomparably copious that its echo in the normal run of mental life seems dead and abstract. This is why it is unjustly mistaken as unfeeling, cold and remote from reality.

IX   The Idea of Freedom

With an open mind it is possible to observe thinking directly as a self-contained entity. One can live within it, in the inner weavings of its self-sufficient being, for the concrete reality of mind or spirit appears initially to the human being in the form of self-dependent thinking. When thinking is observed, concept and percept are congruent. Not until the percept has been permeated by thinking has the full reality been penetrated. It is through intuition that thinking manifests in consciousness as a self-dependent, spiritually concrete presence. Only through intuition can the essence of thinking be grasped.

The psychosomatic organisation of the human organism has no effect upon the essential nature of thinking. It rather shrinks back and gives ground to thinking. Thinking uses the body to prepare its appearance insofar as it suppresses the activity of the body's organisation and in its place puts itself.

While the "I" is integral to thinking, "I-consciousness" arises through the fact that in the general field of consciousness the traces of thinking activity impress themselves like footprints in soft ground.

In order to gain some insight into the relationship between thinking, the conscious Self and the action of the will we will describe how an action of the will arises in the human organism.

As a determinant of will activity, the volitional motif is a momentary representational, conceptual factor, in contrast to the more permanent forces that drive the will. People will be motivated differently according to their individual character. This is why volitional motifs have different effects. It is these character-based variations in the effects of motifs that distinguishes one person's behaviour from another's. My character is formed by the content of my thoughts and feelings. According to the nature of this content, a particular thought or concept will make me feel inclined or disinclined to do something, and this will in turn become a motif for a particular action, or not as the case may be. A percept can immediately become a volitional motif, without the intervention of a feeling or a concept. This is the case with the instinctive drives. When direct perception of hunger, thirst or sexual desire sets the will in motion, this can be designated as the first level of individual life.

The same goes for social habits, as when we perform a conventional action in response to a particular perception without thinking about it or feeling anything much.

A second level of human life comes to light when feelings linked to external percepts become the mainsprings of action. Among these are modesty, pride, humility, regret, pity, revenge or duty.

Thirdly, volitional motifs can be formed by means of thinking and visualisation – when, for instance, out of experience of the perception of certain things we visualise certain actions, which we have carried out under similar circumstances, or have seen someone else carry out.

As the fourth and highest level, conceptual thinking may also engender motifs without any recourse to a particular perception. Here pure thinking becomes the mainspring of action. This applies to action under the influence of intuition. Here the motivation is no longer merely individual, but stems from the ideal, and therefore, universal content of my intuition.

Both external authorities, such as family, state or church, and inner ones, such as conscience, can determine our actions. It signifies progress, when we are not merely following the dictates of an external or internal authority, but the attempt is being made to gain insight as to why a certain action should ensue. Actions like this are performed not out of moral authority, but out of moral insight. The highest conceivable principle of morality arises out of the pure spring of intuition and has no immediate relationship to perception. In this connection only the ideas relating to an act of will contribute to its motif. All other determinants take second place, and thus the primary candidate for the role of highest motif is idea-driven intuition. Motivation and motif are then identical. Such an action does not occur in any stereotyped or automatic way, or according to pre-written rules, but is determined solely by its ideal content.

This kind of action is predicated upon our being capable of moral intuition. Without the ability to discern the moral maxim appropriate to each special case there is no genuinely individual will. Kant's view of this was different. He stipulated that the principles of individual action could be formulated so as to be equally valid for everyone. This, of course, renders individually motivated action impossible. To do what anyone would do in any particular instance cannot be the standard of conduct; the thing is, rather, to do what is right for me.

People differ in terms of their capacity for intuition. One person has no shortage of ideas, another has to work hard to acquire them. People also have different life-worlds. Accordingly each person's world of ideas is differently constituted, and thus determines the constellation of ideas at work in him, the actual content of his intuition. The highest mainspring of morality is the giving of free rein to this action-oriented store of intuition. This standpoint may be called *ethical individualism*.

An intuitively determined act is distinguished by finding the individual intuition that corresponds to the concrete case in point. The motivation for such an act does not arise from norms or rules, but from a moral maxim which has its place in my intuition and is connected with my love for whatever it is I am trying to achieve with the act. I can be said to carry out an act of this kind once I have conceived the idea of it without asking anyone for permission, or consulting a rule as to whether I should do it. It is entirely my act, because I follow my love of its purpose, without submitting to any inner or outer authority. The act will be "good" if my love-filled intuition is in harmony with what can be intuitively experienced of the state of affairs to which it applies. Otherwise it will be "evil". An act of this kind is not under any compulsion, from nature, from desire or from moral statutes. My inclination is the sole arbiter of what happens.

It is true, of course, that the criminal acts out of his individuality. His motivations, however, do not arise from intuitively experienced elements of the universal world of ideas, but from instincts and drives belonging to the extra-ideal generality of the human world.

A free act, on the other hand, can only arise from the ideal aspects of my individual being. Only the human being is free, endowed with the capability of being his own guide at any moment of his life. Freedom of action incorporates the moral laws within its purview; but it is a higher form of action than that dictated by such laws. The free individual is no longer dependent upon a fixed moral order. Such general norms are justified while human beings are still not capable of finding an intuitive basis for their actions in the world of ideas. This world of ideas has universal validity. This is why there can be no misunderstandings between individuals who are taking their inspiration from there. The free human being lives in the love of action and in tolerant understanding of the intentions of others. Because all human individuals are one in the spirit they are able to live their different lives side by side. The free individual trusts that she belongs to the same spiritual world as the other free individuals and that their intentions will therefore coincide.

A human being can only become a free individual through personal effort. Society forms him into a law-abiding individual. Up to this stage of life rules and laws are justified. Beyond it, the human being must take responsibility for his own development. Free spirituality is the final stage of human development, and not until we are free are we truly human.

X   The philosophy of freedom and
      monism

From the naïve realist's point of view, for
which only sense data are valid, moral life
must also be based purely upon the sense-
perceptible. It begins by taking the word of a
single individual, then progresses to that of a
majority, for instance, the state or society.
The next highest level would be that of some
supra-human power, which will be pictured
with sense-perceptible features, for instance,
as an embodied deity. At the highest level of
naïve realism's approach to morality, the
moral precept is seen as an absolute inner
power. Thus it becomes a self-existent meta-
physical entity. If, however, this entity is
considered to be devoid of thought, operat-
ing according to purely mechanical laws, as
would be the case with a materialist way of
thinking, then all my actions would be merely the result of the material processes under-
lying my bodily and mental organisation,
and freedom an illusion. The dualist
worldview sees the extra-human absolute in

a spiritual being that stands behind the appearances, and thus seeks the motivation for will activity in this sort of absolute spiritual power. Accordingly, the human being does not act because she wills it, but because she has to act in the interest of this extra-human being.

For monism the idea is synonymous with the percept. The idea can appear within a person's mind and he can then feel free in following it as motivation. The human being is free when he obeys himself, unfree when he follows the dictates of a perceived external compulsion. From a monistic point of view the human being is at first unfree in the sense-perceptible world she finds herself in, and comes then to the realisation of herself as a free individual. Then, rejecting the extraneous, she puts into practice her own decisions and intentions. Insofar as she brings intuitive ideas to realisation, she no longer pursues any outside purposes, but only her own. Someone acting under physical or moral compulsion cannot be truly moral in her own right. Acting out of automatic, instinctive impulse or in obedience to norms is a necessary preliminary stage in the development of morality, but the free individual transcends this. Freedom is morality in truly human form.

The experience of thinking has the same general features for everyone. The ideas arrived at by thinking, however, express themselves differently in the individual mind. This is not a contradiction, for in gaining knowledge of the world of ideas each person is entering into experience of its universal validity. He individualises a part of this ideal world when he borrows from it the intuitions for an act of will.

XI   The purpose of the world and the purpose of life

Before doing something, the human being represents the action in his mind. As regards its purpose, the act, as something that occurs later, affects – via the representation process – the earlier, in this case, the person about to perform the act.

With cause and effect the situation is reversed. Here a previous event determines a later one. Cause and effect are contiguous in the mind, if we are not in a position to combine the appropriate concepts with one another. Not until the cause has been perceived can the effect follow. The effect can only exert an actual influence upon the cause by means of the conceptual factor, for before the perceptual factor of the cause, that of the effect does not exist. This is why, in relation to nature, we cannot say that the purpose of the blossom is the root, in other words, that the blossom has an influence upon the root. To do so is only possible through what can be construed of the blossom by thinking, in other words, through a contribution from the world of ideas. Due to the fact that here – in contrast to the situation with human action – the cause is not actually influenced by a perceptible process, the concept of purpose cannot be applied. Thus the naïve realist mistakenly believes that the Creator makes organisms according to the same teleological patterns by which we make tools and machines. In philosophical terms it is equally impossible to accept the notion of an extra-worldly world-purpose, or that the purpose of the human being is extra-humanly determined. The concept of purpose only applies to human action. Nature has laws, but not purposes. Similarly, the human being only has purpose insofar as she determines it herself. She sets her own tasks in life. In relation to nature it is not possible to speak of purpose, because its determining ideas do not act from outside, but from within her creatures. The creatures of nature are not functionally determined from outside, for instance, according to the plan of a Creator, but causally and lawfully from within.

In rejecting the notion that the essential reality of the universe is absolute, unknowable and only susceptible to hypothetical models, the reason for assuming purpose in nature falls away. This does not imply that all events are the result of purely natural causes. The concept of purpose is to be rejected in relation to a spiritual world lying outside human action, because in this spiritual world something of a higher nature is revealed than a purpose confined to manifestation in the human world.

XII   Moral Imagination

The free individual acts according to his own initiative. This will be based on intuitions selected, after due thought, from the comprehensive sum of his ideas. His decisions will thus be absolutely new. In making them he will not be concerned what others did in the particular case or what orders they gave. His reasons for singling out of the totality of his concepts this specific one for translation into action are purely ideal. The action, however, belongs to perceptible reality; in other words, it is in effect identical with a particular percept. Thus the concept has to come to expression in a single concrete event. The mediator between the concept and the percept is the representation. With the unfree individual the motifs of action are immediately available to the mind as representations. He acts in terms of models or received rules. Laws regulate what he does and does not do. He follows them because he is told they carry heavy consequences, such as punishment or damnation, if they are not obeyed. The source of the free individual's action is moral imagination, by means of which he puts his ideas into practice, thus becoming morally productive.

Through what she chooses to do the human being does not create new percepts, but impacts already existing ones. In order to transform a particular percept, she must understand how it is ordered, and find the appropriate mode in which this order can be transformed. The ability to transform the world of percepts without contravening any of the natural laws involved in them is the moral equivalent of engineering. In contrast to the laws of nature, moral laws are made by us. Once this has been done they can be applied and passed on. An individual's moral ideas are likely to have gained her attention from among those of her forefathers. Only when she has moral ideas of her own, however, can she be said to be morally effective. The moral order can be derived from causes within the world of experience. It is in the true nature of a moral act that it is not fully accounted for in being traced back to a supernatural, divine influence, be it a revelation like the Ten Commandments or the appearance of God on earth. The effect of all this upon and within the human being does not become truly moral until she has consciously incorporated it into her experience and made it her own.

The causes of moral processes must be sought in the human being, the carrier of morality. Moral-free life is a spiritual continuation of organic life.

If the human will brings pure, ideal intuitions to realisation, it is free. The human being feels an act to be free, when he experiences it as an image of an ideal intuition. I am free when, through the moral imagination behind my actions, I am able to form representations of my own, in other words, produce them myself instead of taking my moral cues from outside myself. He who is driven by extraneous motifs is unfree in his actions. To the extent that the human being succeeds, in his will activity, in realising within himself the state that arises through the conscious expressing of purely ideal intuitions, he is free.

XIII   The value of life

For optimists this is the best of all possible worlds and living in it of inestimable value. Pessimists, on the other hand, see existence as a burden, and for them non-existence is to be preferred to existence under all circumstances, because the sum of all pain far outweighs that of pleasure.

The value of life, however, cannot be determined simply by looking at the balance-sheet of pain and pleasure. If a desired goal is not achieved, this creates distress, but the joy of the chase in pursuing it must be counted as a pleasure. If a feeling of pleasure turns out later to be an illusion, the period before the disillusionment cannot be regarded as pain. Reason alone is not in a position to make a final judgment about the relative proportions of pain and pleasure. Opting for the predominance of one or the other would have to be based on real-life observation, and testing the calculations against the facts. It may well just not be true that we make the value of life dependent upon how much pain or pleasure we feel. If we were primarily predisposed to strive for pleasure – which, according to pessimists, is ultimately unattainable – then, in fact, it would be more worthwhile striving for non-existence than for existence. Assuming we made the value of life dependent on an excess of pleasure, then every will-impulse that brought us an excess of pain would be worthless. The greater the amount of need and the lesser the enjoyment, the less the impulse would be satisfied. Thus, given a constant level of enjoyment, as a living creature's needs increase, so its pleasure in life will decrease. This goes for the life of nature in general. In life the value of a pleasure is measured in relation to needs. Pleasure is measured on the scale of desires. The degree of pleasure has its full value when its expression and duration exactly coincide with our desire. If in the case of an increasing volume of pleasure our desire does not keep pace, pleasure will switch to its opposite. Too much of an otherwise pleasurable feeling becomes pain. Our desires are not abstract, but concrete, and can therefore only be satisfied in specific ways – hunger, for example, can only be satisfied by eating and not by going for a walk. If the resistance to the fulfilment of a desire is greater than the desire itself and ultimately insuperable, then the desire will wane and the urge to fulfil it will cease. If however fulfilment is achieved after putting up with a hard struggle, the pleasure is likely to be greater than if it had simply happened without any effort. All living creatures will keep their drives in play for as long as they can manage to endure the ensuing pain and distress. The gauge of the will is not the ratio of pleasure and pain, but the desire which carries through as long as it can. The value of pleasure is not determined by how much is left after the associated pain has been subtracted, but by whether the value persists in spite of any pain occasioned. Human action is founded upon the hope of possible satisfaction after all difficulties have been overcome. From this hope springs every individual's engagement in the work they do, and the whole enterprise of cultural activity. Moral duties too are concrete natural and spiritual impulses, seeking satisfaction in spite of associated difficulties and disinclinations. Moral ideals arise out of the human being's moral imagination. They are his intuitions, volitional motifs drawn out from his innermost being, which he wants to actualise, since their actualisation is for him the supreme pleasure. This actualisation of his ideals is an enjoyment, compared with which the pleasure he might get from the satisfaction of every-day desires is very meagre. In seeking thus, out of his own motivation, to unfold human nature to its full and true extent, the human being is attempting to actualise the Good, without following any rules or having to be persuaded into it by any philosophical considerations. Freedom is not expressed through acting out of empirical or emotional necessity, but out of spiritual intuitions.

XIV   Individuality and genus

Every human being belongs to groups of various kinds, through which certain parts of her being are subject to certain influences. Such groups are, for instance, nation, family or gender. Each person has, in the course of her development, the possibility of gradually freeing herself from such group influences, and of developing qualities and functions traceable to no-one but herself. For her, then, group characteristics become merely a medium for the expression of her individual being. Besides whatever genus concepts apply to a person, what must be taken into account in order to understand them fully are those individual idiosyncrasies that can only be explained in personal terms and not in terms of any group membership. Defining an individual according to the characteristics of the group she belongs to reaches its limit where the realm of freedom of thought and action begins. What an individual is to think cannot, therefore, be derived solely from group characteristics. Human individuality can only be partially understood by a science based on all-embracing group-related concepts, and that only insofar as those concepts apply to the person concerned. In connection with those aspects of a person that are free of the influences of a particular group we cannot make use of abstract ideas and group concepts in explaining her thoughts and actions. A free individual can only be understood by our being able to accurately apprehend the self-defining concepts she has adopted as her own. Within a human community only that part of a human being's make-up which she has freed from group influence can be regarded as individually free. No one is wholly group-determined, nor exclusively individual. But only those aspects of her actions that arise from her intuitions and are thus free of the influences and constraints of a group have true ethical value. All the results of moral imagination generated by free individuals together form the moral life of humanity. This is the outcome of monism.

The consequences of monism

Everything needed to explain the world can be derived from human experience. The springs of action too are to be sought within observable human nature, namely, within our moral nature. Thought-filled empirical observation brings unity to the multiplicity of percepts, and via this unity the human urge for knowledge seeks entry into the world's physical and spiritual realms. Only for our perception is the connection between the human individual and the whole of the cosmos interrupted. This apparent separateness turns out to be a mere illusion once what has been perceived is integrated through intuitive thinking into the web of the world of ideas. The human being only discovers the self-contained unity of the universe by intuitive thinking, which destroys the illusion created by perception and integrates us as individuals into the life of the cosmos. Thinking spans the subjective and objective at the same time, and in the fusion of percept and concept full reality is delivered. The abstract form of the concept is purely subjective, but not the concept filled with content gained from being drawn from reality by thinking and combined with the percept. This content is a mode of experience not mediated by perception. Our intellectual organisation tears reality in two – namely, the factors of abstract concept and percept. Full reality is the complementary relationship between them, the percept being integrated into the order of the universe. The mere percept in itself presents observation with a meaningless chaos. On the other hand, the process of observation on its own delivers us merely abstract concepts. It is only once observation is permeated with thinking that we get reality, which encompasses both concept and percept in concrete combination. Only when we find the ideas that relate to the percepts do we live in reality, and then we do not have to search for a higher reality outside our world of experience. The real, in absolute terms, lies within what can be experienced intuitively, and the content of experience is thus knowledge of the real. This process of knowing grasps reality in its true form, not as a subjective image.

The conceptual content of the world is the same for all human individuals, and in the mind of every individual the same world content is in play. For every specific percept there is only one concept for each perceiving subject to call upon. All perceiving subjects are led by their thinking towards the common ideal unity. To turn his inner gaze into the all-encompassing world of ideas is for the human being to see the living absolute, the real, lighting up within him. Thinking enables me to see that other people have access to the same world of ideas as I do. In his thinking the individual grasps only a part of this ideational whole, and consequently people differ as regards the actual content of their thinking. But the thought content of all human beings is encompassed in one self-contained whole. In his thinking the individual person is subject to the active presence of the universal primordial Being that pervades all human beings. To live in reality filled with the content of thought is at the same time to live in God. *This* world has the foundation of its existence within itself. All inferences about a beyond that are not based on thought-filled experience are projected abstractions of one kind or another. The God assumed by such abstraction, for instance, is just a human being transplanted into the beyond. The human mind can rest content in *this* world, for it contains everything required to explain it. Also the goals of human action are not to be derived from some assumed extra-human Beyond. Rather it is up to each person to decide for himself what the focus of his actions should be. If he goes beyond simply seeking to satisfy his natural drives and instincts, he will have to seek the motivation for the actions of his will by means of his own moral imagination, or permit himself the convenience of being guided by the moral imagination of others. If he succeeds in getting beyond his sensual drives and obeying the orders of others, then he will be completely self-determined – acting entirely on his own motivation, which is, of course, ultimately determined by the one world of ideas. Only in the human being is to be found the basis upon which ideas can be turned into reality. Before an idea appears in action, this must be willed by a human being. Such will activity has its foundation only in the human being. The human being is the ultimate judge of his own actions, and thus he is *free*.

Key thoughts for each chapter

I:

The act illuminated by thought is a different act.

II:

Apprehending nature in oneself means that she can be discovered outwardly as well, for within and around us the one world holds sway.

III:

Thoughtfully observe thinking, in order to understand it and everything else along with it.

IV:

Thinking connects us to the world, it distinguishes and combines, encapsulates and orders the perceptible.

V:

Thinking awakens out of mere perception, integrates us into the whole, for only with thinking are being and appearance one and the same.

VI:

Human existence is universal through thinking, individual through feeling.

VII:

The realms of percept and concept are united by thinking to form reality.

VIII:

In unconstrained, living thinking, feeling and will are also present.

IX:

Once the ideational component of an act is known, it can be carried out in freedom.

X:

To follow the pure idea means to act without compulsion, in other words, in freedom.

XI:

The purpose of a human being can only be decided by himself.

XII:

If I apprehend and determine the reasons for what I intend, then my action will be free.

XIII:

Pleasure derived from the satisfaction of a drive is limited and meagre in comparison to the spiritual enjoyment that flows from a freely made decision.

XIV:

Not commandments, but free intuitions determine truly ethical action.